GETTING BACK
AT THE TRAFFIC WARDEN
Introducing WTW Doris de Sade

...ton

Additional Research by Kevin Austin
Cartoons by Derek Hazeldine

Angry driver ran over traffic warden

By GEOFFREY LAKEMAN

A TRAFFIC warden was run down by a motorist he turned away from a car park queue.

William Bennett bowled over warden Len Brown pinning him under the car. Then he reversed, swerved past as Mr. Brown lay injured, and drove into the park.

Later he told another warden. "I'm fed up with you bastards."

And he was still so enraged when police arrived that he had to be hauled away in handcuffs.

Yesterday, Mr. Brown told Exeter Court that Bennett 48, of nearby Exwick, refused to move on after being asked not to join a long queue for the car park.

He said: "Suddenly I felt a bump on my leg. It was the front bumper and the pressure was building up.

"The car pushed me to the ground until my legs were under the front. I was terrified."

When police were called and Bennett was told he had knocked the warden he replied: "What a load of crap—he should have got out of the way."

Bennett's lawyer told magistrates: "He has this enormous aggression against wardens. He clearly has a problem."

The court heard that Bennett had a previous conviction for assaulting a warden and had also been accused of harassing learner drivers.

He was convicted of assault, reckless driving and failing to stop and was remanded in custoday for reports.

Daily Mirror, 1st May 1984.

The Nature of the Beast

A glance at the news report on the left, published in the Daily Mirror on May 1st, 1984, should be all that is needed for drivers and Traffic Warden haters anonymous to realise that <u>violent</u> remedies do not work – even on May Day!

Consider the penalty for this slight nudge in a car park. The book was very thoroughly thrown at the offending driver. Assault, reckless driving <u>and</u> failing to stop – plus remanded pending reports. Bet he also got the bill for cleaning the Traffic Warden's trousers! There must be a reason for this – and there is.

Drivers who rise early might observe dark blue police vans dropping off Traffic Wardens at strategic starting points in the urban area. One could be forgiven for thinking that the police had locked up all the Traffic Wardens overnight for their own protection, releasing them very carefully one at a time the following morning to guard against any risk of another Brixton riot.

This is not so, Traffic Wardens are, in fact, allied to, in constant communication with, and the responsibility of the police force. So, be warned. Doing things nasty to a Traffic Warden is akin to doing things nasty to the Fuzz. Same man hunt; same national publicity; same maximum penalties.

Subtler, non-violent ways must be employed. But before chronicling these, let us first study the make-up of this strange body who would take on the world and such an anti-social job as a Traffic Warden.

EYES: ULTRAVIOLET ASSISTED, THEY CAN SEE THROUGH A DODGY EXCUSE IN A BLINK.

NOSE: SIMILAR IN SHAPE TO THE NOSE CONE OF AN RAF NIMROD AND JUST AS POWER-PACKED. IT CAN DETECT A PARKING VIOLATOR AT UP TO 7 MILES - THROUGH CONCRETE AND STEEL.

HANDS: WHEN NOT HANDING OUT TICKETS, CLASPED FIRMLY BEHIND THE BACK - THE RESULT OF POLICE TRAINING.

BAG: CONTAINS AN INEXHAUSTIBLE SUPPLY OF PARKING TICKETS, PLASTIC ENVELOPES, PENS AND SELLOTAPE **PLUS** EMERGENCY RATIONS IN CASE OF ABDUCTION, A SWISS ARMY KNIFE AND 6 RIOT GAS GRENADES.

CAP: THE SHAPE FAVOURED BY HITLER'S BLACKSHIRTS - A FAIR GUIDE TO WHAT GOES ON IN THE BRAIN BENEATH.

SMILE: WHEN FACED WITH THIS RARE PHENOMENON TRY 0-60 IN 3 SECONDS.

RADIO: BE WARNED! THIS IS A DIRECT LINK WITH THE LOCAL NICK.

TIE: CLIP-ON, TO THWART ANY ATTEMPT AT STRANGULATION.

HEART: IF A T.W. EVER NEEDS A TRANSPLANT THE DONOR WILL HAVE TO BE A VERY LARGE, STRIPED, FOUR-LEGGED PREDATOR.

LEGS: EAT YOUR HEART OUT, DALEY THOMPSON!

FOOTWEAR: TOO CLOSE FOR COMFORT TO S.S. JACKBOOTS!

Little is known about the recruitment process for Traffic Wardens. Advertisements headed "Traffic Wardens Required" are rare indeed.

It is as if the powers that be seek suitable candidates from the ranks of those who have already passed through their hands and whose whereabouts are still known.

Our researcher, Kevin Austin, who is a very able and bodied young man, sought at his local police headquarters to fill any suitable vacancies, but failed the lie detector test.

From all the data we have gleaned, we have pieced together the arch-typical recruitment advertisement which we present on page 7.

NOW DON'T FORGET, GIRLS, NO FRATERNIZING WITH THE ENEMY!

Traffic Wardens Required

Lonely? Chip on your shoulder? Frustrated in your quest for POWER? We've got just the job for you.

Male, female or transvestite. Any colour and ethnic origin. Must be fit and capable of walking 30 miles a day in all weathers. Must hate people, especially shoppers, salesmen and delivery drivers.

Preference will be given to applicants who are disbarred accountants or dentists, tax inspectors or VAT officers, disqualified-for-life drivers, members of Militant Tendancy or the National Front, rape victims, survivors of broken marriages, lifelong spinsters and relatives of Arthur Scargill.

Weekly wage plus 10% commission on all fixed penalties over target. Profit sharing scheme on unclaimed towed away vehicles. Free personal accident and life insurance, uniform, three pairs of Toetectors per month and comprehensive training in self-defence.

Apply to Chief Inspector Booker, Traffic Department, Police Headquarters, Warmonger Street.

8

Be Nice to your Local Traffic Warden

Being nice to other people ALWAYS pays better dividends than being nasty – even when the other people are Traffic Wardens.

Bill Bradley is a salesman. He visits stores and offices in his local area, calling on most of his customers three or four times a month. He drives an ordinary kind of saloon of an ordinary kind of colour.

Bill regularly parks in places he shouldn't, rather risking the penalty than risking the order by being late for an appointment through trying to find a legal place to park. Yet Bill rarely gets parking tickets.

He puts his success down to what he calls his "Pip and Wave" technique. Driving around his area, whenever he passes a Traffic Warden, he pips his horn and waves.

The thought process of the Traffic Warden goes "Who the hell was that?" Second time Bill's Pip and Wave technique is used, thought process continues – "There's that guy again. He obviously knows me. Who the devil is he? I don't recognise the car."

Third time, the Traffic Warden waves back. Several pips later, Bill's car is encountered in a forbidden place. Traffic Warden recognises car. "Here's that unknown friend of mine. I'll hang around a while and see if he comes back. Then at least I'll know who he is."

If Bill, on the way back to his car, sees the Traffic Warden nearby, he makes another call. Ten minutes later, the Traffic Warden has grown tired of waiting and has started on another circuit. Bill finishes extra call and re-joins car. Still no parking ticket and twice his expected illegal wait.

NOW DON'T YOU STAY HERE ALL DAY, YOU NAUGHTY BOY.

No jokes, you're a traffic warden

Sunday Mirror Reporter

GRUMPY police chiefs are threatening to throw the book at jolly Ann Price, the Laughing Traffic Warden.

They are laying down the law because she went out on street duty wearing a garland of flowers round her peaked hat.

It wasn't the first time amused motorists and shoppers at Woodstock in Oxfordshire had seen Ann getting up to her tricks. She once went looking for outlaw parkers wearing a Wild West sheriff's badge on her hat.

Now senior officers from Thames Valley Police have cautioned her. They say she'll be sacked if there are any more pranks. Ann has been transferred to nearby Witney.

One Woodstock trader said: "We shall miss Ann. You never knew what she was going to get up to next."

Ann, 43, wore the floral garland after Woodstock was criticised in a national garden competition for being short of flowers.

Smiling Ann, who lives in Witney, said: "I enjoy life, but I don't think I brought the traffic warden's job into disrepute. There were no complaints that I didn't book enough people."

A police spokesman said: "Obviously you can't have a uniformed person wandering about with flowers in their hair. The public must be able to look upon officers such as traffic wardens as figures of authority with a proper sense of dignity."

Traffic Wardens who want to bring a bit of cheer to their "customers", like jolly Ann Price of Witney, get it in the neck from their police superiors.

A Warden in Warwick who was a fanatical sports car enthusiast (Yes, some of them actually drive!) was fired for spending too much of his duty time under the bonnet of local sports cars, drooling over the works while their owners went about their business.

One local traveller, who wishes to remain anonymous, has taken Bill Bradley's "Pip and Wave" technique and added icing to the cake.

On the logical assumption that a Traffic Warden is hardly likely to book another Traffic Warden, he keeps a Traffic Warden's cap on his front passenger seat. Local Warden finds car parked in the wrong zone; recognises car belonging to unknown friend. Looks inside and sees cap on front seat. Thinks "It's one of us from another area".

11

Rental Cars Rarely Attract Parking Tickets

Cy Steidler, advertising executive, found his favourite ticket beating gambit by accident. On holiday with his wife in a strange city, he parked his rented car between two others and spent a happy hour souvenir shopping.

The Air Force corporal walking up the road didn't register in Cy's thoughts until same Air Force corporal began writing out tickets and sticking them on car windscreens. "Hey, Nancy, they dress Traffic Wardens different over here. Looks like we're going to get booked."

Now Cy is an old campaigner. He's been renting cars on his overseas trips for years and parking them where the hell he likes, confident in the knowledge that he'll be long gone before any parking ticket percolates through the system towards him.

But he doesn't stick his neck out unduly. So he and Nancy stayed in the souvenir shop until the Warden had disappeared. Across the road to his rental car – to find it was still virgin. No ticket! Yet the cars fore and aft were festooned.

And then the truth dawned. Traffic Wardens aren't so dumb as to waste their time booking a <u>Rental</u> car. They know full well the driver will be long gone before the paperwork gets going.

So back home, Cy placed some Rental brochures on the parcel shelf of his <u>own</u> car, added a Rental sticker to front and rear screen, another on each bumper, and tested the theory out for his home patch driving.

So far, he reports plenty of illegal parking and no tickets.

13

Loading and Unloading

To take advantage of the preferential treatment normally awarded to drivers who are legitimately loading or unloading in the course of their business, the right kind of vehicle is desirable.

Drivers who've bought a second hand hearse will need to dress to fit the part, and their goods will need to be carried in a rather conspicuous container.

Rolls Royce drivers have little scope, but at least they should be able to afford to pay the fine.

Arthur Forbes drives your ordinary kind of saloon. In seeking to develop a "loading and unloading" technique for weekend shopping, he quickly found that "shopping", however bulky or heavy, was not considered by Traffic Wardens as grounds for the granting of privileges.

Thus, his shopping had to be disguised as something more business-like. He acquired two identical cardboard boxes from a company that supplied cash registers to shops. Each box was clearly labelled "Acme Cash Register".

Parked on a single yellow line, ready for a shopping spree, his car boot stays open with one of the cardboard boxes inside it. All normal boot items are at home or locked inside the car. The other cardboard box goes with Arthur and wife, to be filled with shopping. Arthur carries full box, top closed, back to car. Wife hovers a few yards back. If the coast is clear, both board and drive away. If a Traffic Warden is adjacent, Arthur loads full box into boot, picks up empty box, making like it's heavy, says to the Traffic Warden – "Cash register's gone haywire. Got to replace it. Shan't be more than five minutes." Shuts car boot so that Traffic Warden can't examine the full box, and walks back into shop. Wife hovers until Traffic Warden is safe distance away, then signals to Arthur, who returns to car with empty box and both drive away.

Drivers with estate cars or vans can add a very useful tool to the boxes idea. A sack truck. Resting against a tail gate, with a delivery man's clipboard lying just inside the vehicle, it is proof positive that the driver is engaged on legitimate business.

Kennel Club

Clive and Janice Jones run a kennels and kattery. They drive an estate car fitted out for carrying animals to and from kennels and customers. Many of their regular customers are flat dwellers in congested areas.

Time and again, while collecting or delivering a pet, Clive and Janice's estate car was booked for illegal parking. They lived in an area full of very keen Traffic Wardens.

The number of tickets became unbearable. A drain on their business's profits. So they decided to train one of their own pets – an Irish Wolfhound – to perform a very specific function.

The estate car was given an extra grill, so that the tailgate could be left open without the animals inside escaping. The Wolfhound lay on the last two feet of the estate section. It was a loveable, docile animal, except in one respect. Clive and Janice had trained it to guard their car against attack by Traffic Wardens.

Any Warden who stopped by the estate car caused the hound to bound from the tailgate and stand growling, hackles up and teeth bared. No offensive action. Merely defence. But no Traffic Warden was prepared to take a chance on that.

Heavies

Of course, if the driver's chariot is a HGV, he is several miles above the field. The Traffic Warden doesn't even THINK of shopping sprees when encountering a 32 ton artic tractor in the High Street.

Bert Figgins is a long distance lorry driver. Self-employed. Owns his own tractor, complete with sleeping cab, which is another story! The tractor, without its usual container trailer, is not much more in length than your average saloon car. And much easier to park. Nobody ever argues with a Heavy!

Bert takes the wife shopping in his tractor every Saturday. He hangs a polite little notice in his cab window to keep the Traffic Wardens sweet. Most times, they can't even reach the tractor's windscreen to affix a ticket. Most times, they don't even try.

Sudden Emergencies

How many Traffic Wardens would be sympathetic towards the driver who leaves a hurried, hand-written note on the windscreen, which reads:

SORRY. HAD TO DASH
TO FIND A TOILET.
BACK AS FAST AS I CAN.

Salesman Jack Duncan uses this gambit when he needs to improperly park his car to keep an important appointment. In early "trials" he found the note worked some of the time, but not every time.

He found the "every time" answer in a joke shop. A very realistic looking pool of sick, made of yellowish brown plastic, with chunks of chewed and partially digested food embedded within it. (Yuckk!)

Placed on the pavement by the driver's door of his car and no Traffic Warden is in any doubt as to the nature of the emergency. One other thing is absolutely guaranteed – no Traffic Warden, or anyone else, is going to check whether that pool of sick is for real or just a plastic replica.

One hundred percent success for Jack Duncan.

I'LL BE BACK IN HALF AN HOUR – IF YOU HAVEN'T SORTED IT OUT BY THEN, I'M BOOKING YOU!

Breakdowns

Want to <u>really</u> fool a Traffic Warden? Jack up the side of the car, take a wheel off, lock it in the boot and go do the business.

Fred Price is a member of the notorious County Bachelors drinking and mayhem club. Bragging one evening about how easy it would be to hoodwink a Traffic Warden, he found himself on the wrong end of a silly bet.

Loosing face is a sin far worse than losing pants to a County Bachelor, so Fred duly set out to honour – and win – the bet.

The task before him was to stage a breakdown in his local High Street, on double yellow lines, for two hours during a peak shopping Saturday, without being lent assistance, towed away or told to get the hell out of there by a Traffic Warden or anyone else. The twist was that the van should stand alone, no human being in attendance, during the whole of the two hours – and the entire proceedings had to be videoed for playback at the next CB party night.

Fred set about his project with the dedication and detailed planning of an SAS commander. A beat up Transit van was selected for the event, borrowed from a local parcels carrier. Equipment included a professional garage trolley jack with pump handle, two tool boxes full of spanners, various greasy mechanical parts from underneath a similar Transit van, a pair of greasy blue mechanic's overalls, a pair of size 11 cheap, oily black boots, socks to match, a portable, battery driven cassette player with auto reverse, an old fashioned hearing aid, complete with lead and ear piece, two plastic red and white road cones – and the bottom half of a male tailor's dummy.

8.45am one cold, wet Saturday morning (Fred had checked the weather forecasts. A warm, sunny day was not part of the plan). Transit and Fred drove into position in the High Street. Opposite, the proprietor of a TV shop, himself a County Bachelor, set up in his shop window a video camera, focusing on the van and locking the camera in position. A VCR unit inside the shop began recording the scene.

Shoppers were not yet out and about. Zero minus 15 minutes!

Fred hauled the trolley jack out of the van, positioned it under the front engine mounting and jacked the front of the van about a foot in the air. Next he pulled the tailor's dummy from the van, already dressed in the greasy mechanic's overalls, oily boots, etc. and slid the dummy under the side of the van, so that the boots and half a foot or so of overall leg was all that could be seen, roadside. Zero minus ten minutes.

Next, the cassette player was placed under the van, adjacent to the torso end of the dummy, and switched on. Fred had spent a happy half hour recording the tape in his garage the weekend before.

The two tool boxes came out next. One was positioned next to the booted feet sticking out the off-side of the van. The other was positioned in front of the van, next to the jack handle. A few spanners were laid onto the road, along with the various greasy mechanical parts from underneath a similar Transit van. Zero minus five minutes.

Two road cones were then placed fore and aft the van. Finally, the most important piece of equipment of all, the hearing aid, was laid out, carefully and conspicuously, on top of the tool box at the front of the van.

Zero minus one minute. Fred took a final, careful look round his set, rubbed his hands with undisguised glee, and sauntered over to the TV shop to his observation post and a cup of coffee.

Saturday shoppers began to bustle. Soon the High Street became congested with people and with traffic. No one took the slightest notice of the broken down van under repair.

At 9.21am a police car drove past the van. The two uniformed occupants looked across at the van, saw the mechanic at work and drove on without stopping.

At 9.43am a Traffic Warden appeared, but on the TV shop side of the High Street. Female, already cold and damp from the morning rain, she stopped and looked across at the van. All appeared in order. Road cones in place and a professional on the job. The Traffic Warden kept walking along the TV shop side of the High Street.

10.37am. The Traffic Warden re-appeared, her usual half hour circuit increased to nearly an hour because of the inclement weather. Again she stopped and looked across at the van. "Obviously a difficult job. Wonder if he needs assistance." She waited for a break in the traffic and crossed the High Street to the van side pavement.

In accordance with standard practice, the Traffic Warden made a complete circuit of the van. She observed that the van belonged to a local carrier. She inspected the jack handle and tool box at the front of the van. She wondered how a hearing aid could help a mechanic repair a vehicle. She looked down at the size 11 oily black boots and the greasy overall legs sticking out from under the van, road side. As she made her inspection she heard the normal kind of spanner noises, clanks and mild swearing coming from beneath the van, intermingling with the humming of one of the County Bachelors' favourite war chants.

Fred's pre-recorded tape was performing well.

The Traffic Warden grimaced at the sight of the greasy mechanical parts which the mechanic had obviously stripped from the van's belly. Clearly this was going to be a long job. She raised her voice to compete against the traffic. "Need any help?" No response from under the van. The spanner noises, swearing and humming continued. "NEED ANY HELP DOWN THERE?" The Traffic Warden shouted.

Still no response. Across the High Street, Fred crossed his fingers. This was the weakest link in his plan. Would the Traffic Warden put two and two together and come up with five? Would she throw away months of rigid training and stoop down to look under the van? He prayed for a below average intelligence level and an above average ego level. His prayer was answered.

Shouting in the High Street was definitely beneath the dignity of a Traffic Warden. Standard procedure took over. Hands clasped behind her back she made another complete circuit of the van. At the front, her eyes once more made contact with the hearing aid on top of the tool box. "Of course," she exclaimed silently, "The man's deaf. That's why he didn't answer me."

Across the High Street, Fred saw the Traffic Warden's head nod twice as she looked at the hearing aid. He hugged himself. It was going to work.

The Traffic Warden made a third circuit of the van, trying to decide what best to do, paused on the pavement, looked hard at her watch, looked up at the rain-filled sky, thought to herself, "Who needs the aggro?" and continued on her rounds.

Much hilarity ensued in the TV shop. Fred looked at <u>his</u> watch.

"Twelve minutes to go. We're practically in the clear."

At 11.05am, Fred left the TV shop and crossed to his van. First item to go back inside the van was the tailor's dummy – as fast as it could go. Then the greasy mechanical parts, equally as fast. No point in taking any chances this close to success.

And a precaution well worthwhile, for, as Fred was straightening up from under the van, having retrieved and turned off his cassette player, he saw walking towards him the Traffic Warden, this time accompanied by a police constable.

Fred just had time to put the cassette player into the back of the van and make sure the doors were firmly shut before they were upon him.

"Sorted out the trouble?" the Traffic Warden asked warmly.

Fred was thinking fast. He turned round to face the Traffic Warden and the policeman, and faked a "you startled me" expression.

"SORTED OUT THE TROUBLE?" the Traffic Warden shouted, smiling, six inches from his left ear.

Fred held up a finger, walked round to the front of the van, picked up the hearing aid, plugged the earpiece into his ear, made as if he was turning the aid on, gave it a tap and faced the two officials. "Sorry, can't hear you without this. No good wearing it under the van. Get's in the way. Been here since a quarter to nine. Hell of a job, but okay now. Thanks for letting me get on with the job."

"That's life." said the copper. "This weather, I reckon you've been in the dryest place under there." And he and the Traffic Warden walked on.

28

The Medics

Because Rigsby publicised use of the "Doctor on Call" notice so well in the film "Rising Damp", Traffic Wardens are attuned to non-medical drivers who use this gambit.

One can feel sorry for bona-fide doctors who drive racey sports cars – and there are many – because their bona-fides often get short shrift.

Charlie Osborne made the "Doctor on Call" notice work by adding a few props to the inside of his car. He acquired a white coat and a stethoscope. Laid out on the back seat, they convinced Traffic Wardens that here was a genuine doctor going about his business.

Duncan Makepeace drives a white estate car. He found a second use for his aluminium camera case. He had it sign written with the words "BLOOD – THIS WAY UP", in red of course, and kept the case in plain view in the back of his estate car. He also acquired a Kojak style flashing green lamp from his local disco music shop, which lived on his back seat with the white coat and a stethoscope. The combination, he claimed, was infallible.

"Was" is the operative word, because Duncan, one tumultuous day, drove into a spot of bad luck.

He came upon a road accident minutes after the police had arrived and before the ambulance. The policeman directing the traffic past the accident looked into Duncan's estate car, leapt to the driver's door, opened it and said, "Excuse me Doctor, we need your help."

Duncan was too shocked to think of saying "Sorry, I'm a Vet."

They took him to the cleaners!!

Disabled Drivers

The author of this book, John Fenton, is better known as "The Billy Graham of Selling" for his somewhat evangelical approach to training salespeople. He is also to Traffic Wardens what Blaster Bates is to Demolition, David Gunson is to Air Traffic Control and Freddie Trueman is to Cricket.

His light-hearted after dinner sessions and interludes during serious sales training meetings, on the subject of "How to Avoid Parking Fines", brought him the dubious indirect distinction in the autumn of 1982 of having caused the powers-that-be in three British towns to withdraw all disabled parking privileges for a month.

Since the publication of this book, he claims to have been living secretly somewhere in the South Midlands, grateful that he can afford a chauffeur/minder to help avoid "the enemy".

He also claims to be the only driver still living to have qualified for four wheel clamps in Central London – all at the same time!

In his latest book on Salesmanship, "How to SELL Against Competition", one example of competition beating referred to a salesman who was blessed with a wooden leg.

Now, not many people would reckon a wooden leg was anything to be blessed with, but then, not many people could use a wooden leg to make as much money as this salesman made. He was in a very competitive market that generated regular repeat business. He and a dozen competitors fought for the business. He got most of it because of his wooden leg.

Not sympathy business, although if he was offered any of that he

SHIVER
SHIVER

happily accepted it. No, all he did was use his wooden leg as a focuser and memory jogger.

When he first met a new prospective customer, he sat with his wooden leg straight out to one side, so that the customer could see four inches of polished teak between his deliberately short sock and his trouser turn-up. He'd turned down the offer of switching from polished teak to skin-coloured contoured aluminium years before.

The sight of that four inches of polished teak, he claimed, used to hypnotise the customers. They couldn't take their eyes off it. Ten minutes maximum and the customer couldn't help himself but say:-
"Excuse me asking: but is that <u>really</u> wood?"

"Oh yes!" the salesman would reply, pulling his trouser leg up another six inches and giving the polished teak a rap with his pen. "Copped a packet during the Cyprus crisis."

A few minutes were then spent talking about the leg, problems in damp weather, etc, but the key factor thereafter for business was that the salesman was never forgotten. Securing the first order was easy. And after that, every time the customer wanted to re-order the goods the salesman sold, the wooden leg was the first thing that came into the customer's mind. The other dozen competitors didn't stand a chance. Nothing for the customer to focus attention on.

Needless to say, our wooden legged salesman also sported a disabled driver's sticker. Leg cases find DD stickers easiest to acquire. Head cases are much more difficult. Diligent use of his DD privileges meant the salesman could make more sales calls than his competitors as well as win most times when he was face-to-face, selling.

But just as with "Doctor on Call" notices, Disabled Driver stickers need additional camouflage if they are to convince the Traffic Wardens every time of the legitimacy of the parked vehicle.

A folding wheel chair in the back might do it. Or one half of a pair of crutches. Be careful with white sticks! A steering wheel knob from a fork lift truck would go down well, too.

Joy Smart has a chest problem. One lung out of action and less than one hundred percent performance from the other. In inclement weather she often has trouble breathing. She also travels extensively on business. Doctors therefore advised her to take with her wherever she goes, a nebuliser (kind of oxygen mask like you never have to use on an aircraft) and a cylinder of oxygen.

Two beautiful props to display in her car, backing up a DD sticker. Never a problem.

And don't forget – if a DD sticker is your chosen gambit, LOOK disabled when leaving or returning to the vehicle.

Val Furness shops several times a week at Marks & Spencer. Parking near to the M & S store is next to impossible. Val is a bundle of fun and a consummate actress. She also doesn't like carrying shopping.

So she acquired a DD sticker for her car, an aluminium arm rest stick and a very unhealthy limp. M & S staff are now used to Val and she doesn't even have to ask before one of the male employees volunteers to carry her shopping out to her car.

Val's only source of embarrassment is when one of her friends happens to be walking past as she and her helper come out of the store. "Val! Good heavens! What ever have you done?"

"Shhhhhh!" Val grins back. "I'll give you a ring this evening and tell you about it."

RASP RASP

Council Officials

George Clayton fell over his favourite gambit outside a cafe. He'd parked legally nearby and gone in for a cuppa. When he came out, he observed a rather irate lady arguing with a Traffic Warden over the ticket being fixed to her windscreen.

"But you haven't given that van a ticket," the lady complained, pointing to a white van parked immediately in front of her car, "and it was there when I drove up."

The Traffic Warden shrugged. "That's a Council van. They can park anywhere."

George walked away from the argument, smiling to himself and thinking about the Traffic Warden's words. Did all Traffic Wardens feel the same way about vehicles belonging to the local Council? Were Council officials given preferential treatment when it came to parking?

He decided to test the theory. Being in the building industry, he already had an appropriately dented, originally white, pick-up. He allocated some permanent space, just behind the cab, for some easily acquired props. A stack of four plastic road cones. A stone pitted metal road notice reading "District Council – SURVEYING", a scrap set of temporary traffic lights and a white plastic construction helmet.

A piece of tarpaulin for covering the rest of his load, just in case it clashed with his newly found Council image, and he reckoned he was in business.

Many illicit parking forays later, he still has a ticket free record.

Driver clamps police car

ANGRY motorist John Savile wheel-clamped a police car he found in his rented parking space.

He padlocked his home-made clamp on the panda car—a Ford Fiesta—near his work in Ipswich, Suffolk.

When the driver came back he had to send for two other policemen to help lift the car out of the clamp.

Now John is sending a £5 illegal parking "fine" to the chief constable.

Fed up

The V clamp is made from two old car wheels, a couple of lengths of metal and padlocks.

John said: "I put it together because I was so fed up with other drivers parking their cars in my space.

"There is a notice in the yard warning people that their wheels will be clamped if they park illegally.

"But I never thought I

By PETER KANE

would catch a police car.

"The notice says that the owners of the car will be fined £5 before the vehicle is freed.

"But the bobby wasn't willing to part with his money. So there it stayed.

"It's no more than the law does to hundreds of motorists every day."

Suffolk police said: "One of our cars was unlawfully clamped and we had to send along a couple of officers to rescue a colleague. We do not wish to comment further."

NABBED: Panda car in home-made clamp

Daily Mirror, 21st August 1984.

Wheel Clamps

Wheel clamps are now commonplace in central London, and likely to be extended to other cities. As a deterrent, they are highly effective because it costs the offending driver the best part of half a day to get the vehicle released, and time is money.

Several very rich drivers in London have walked away from their clamped vehicle to the nearest showroom and purchased another car, on principle, leaving the previous motor to the mercies of the towaway team and the pound – forever!

Other, not quite so rich, drivers call up a second car on their radio telephone and give the second car's driver the job of sorting out the clamp release and fine.

Alf Harper is a cockney bookie's collector who has to run the gauntlet of "clampers row" every day to do his job. After a succession of frustrating waits for the release men to turn up, he decided to do something to keep one step (or one clamp) ahead of the clampers.

He commissioned his own personal wheel clamp from a mate who ran a metal fabrication shop. Illicitly parked in the wheel clamp zone, his personal clamp comes out of his car boot and onto his offside wheel.

Alf claims this not only keeps off the official wheel clampers, it

also keeps his car clear of Traffic Warden's tickets. If a Traffic Warden sees a vehicle has already been clamped, a windscreen ticket is rather superfluous.

Gerald Porter, on the other hand, is determined to stamp out the threat of the wheel clamp by making it uneconomical for the powers-that-be to continue with their plans. A master locksmith, he quickly developed all the necessary keys and associated wrenches to unlock a wheel clamp.

Several of his most intimate circle of friends have been introduced to his mews lock-up garage in the backwaters of Chelsea, which is already stacked from floor to ceiling with his collection of wheel clamps.

His is a long term project. He considers his collection an investment. Seven years and one day after the cessation of wheel clamp hostilities (Statute of Limitations) he plans to auction his trophies as "Victoriana of the Big Brother Era."

This loss of several hundred wheel clamps is a subject which elicits from Metropolitan Police spokesmen a tight-lipped "No Comment!" For this "isolated incident" to develop into a new collecting cult would be an economic disaster for the traffic departments of our Metropolis.

Bomb Disposal

It took a retired Army bomb disposal Sergeant to dream up this one.

The recipe begins with one Army surplus short wheelbase Land Rover, still in olive green camouflage.

Add two stacks of plastic road cones (these road cones are the most universally useful Traffic Warden deterrent. £3.50 from your local builders merchant; if you're honest!), two signs reading "BOMB DISPOSAL" and two more signs reading "KEEP AWAY – SUSPECTED EXPLOSIVE DEVICE".

Mix with a heavy flack jacket and an arc-welder's helmet and dark visor.

Colour with a couple of duff World War Two mortar bombs (from any military memorabilia shop) and a coil of rope to which red plastic strips have been knotted every two feet.

Any Traffic Warden noting such a parked vehicle is guaranteed not to come within two hundred yards of it for the rest of its stay. Come to that, the vehicle owner is hardly likely to be shopping in a crowded store, either.

Football Coaches

Running a close second to the Bomb Disposal Land Rover for clearing streets and keeping Traffic Wardens at the other end of town is the Football Coach.

Bloxwich United has a very virile supporters club. One small section of the supporters club, about thirty fans and their spouses, live some ten miles away from the home ground in a neighbouring town. Because the pre and post match festivities are as important to the supporters as the game itself, this happy band of fans and spouses hires a coach to travel to and from the match.

But Saturday is not only match day, it is weekly shopping day. And there is no one like a male football fan a few hours before the match for developing Saturday morning "shopping legs".

So the lads got together and devised a plan. For a nominal extra fee, the coach driver was prepared to start out two hours earlier. For an equally nominal extra fee, the coach was equipped with video TV.

The extra two hours are spent illegally parked right outside the town's main department stores and supermarkets, one after the other. At each stop, the wives descend from the coach and do their Saturday shopping. The majority of the male fans stay with the coach, watching last week's match on the TV. The coach driver is look-out man, checking ahead and in his rear-view mirror for approaching Traffic Wardens.

At a signal from the driver that a Traffic Warden is approaching, windows are opened throughout the coach and football scarves are hung out and waved. The entire band bursts into song with the Bloxwich United attack chant. As the approaching Traffic Warden stops, turns deathly white, then about faces and beats a swift retreat, the attack chant changes to a goal-scoring roar.

Ever since Woman Traffic Warden Mavis Horrocks tried to book a football coach full of hyped-up cup tie supporters outside public toilets at Marble Arch, and was stripped naked, tied to the back of the coach with club scarves and dragged screaming the length of Park Lane – a widely reported event – Traffic Wardens everywhere are known to give Football Coaches a very wide berth indeed.

MUMMY!

♫ YOU'LL NEVER WALK ALONE ♫
WE WON
THE CUP
UNITED RULES!
EMERGENCY EXIT

Brown Wrappers

In CB Radio jargon, Brown Wrappers are unmarked police cars.

The jargon originates from the USA, where one is required to keep to 55 miles per hour for 2000 miles of endless dual carriageway in over-comfortable seats. Without falling asleep. Over there being able to recognise a Brown Wrapper is pretty important.

The author, on three trips to the States, discovered by research and experimentation how American drivers pick out the unmarked police car.

In most States, licence plates (combined registration number and road fund licence) are displayed on the rear of the vehicle only, and include the name of the State in which the vehicle is licenced.

Brown Wrappers only operate within their home State. Thus, first thing to check is that the vehicle being approached fast from the rear corresponds to the State in which one is driving at the time.

All police cars, Brown Wrappers or standard issue, have four doors, one or more radio aerials and one or two male occupants.

So, approaching an in-State licenced, four door, two aerial, two male occupant car, assume the worst until proven wrong.

But better than this is to tack behind a heavy truck travelling at 80 mph. All truckers use sophisticated CB radio. They know precisely where the Brown Wrappers are hiding.

To a Traffic Warden, a British Brown Wrapper (CID style) is a friend and colleague in arms who can park anywhere, any time. So the art of Brown Wrapper Camouflage (BWC) has been developed to a very advanced stage.

A few years back, during the time the Police Federation, the force's trade union, was campaigning strongly for more pay for our coppers, it was easy. Apply to the local Police Federation secretary for a campaign sticker, designed for the rear window of the car. The sticker read:-

UP POLICE PAY – DOWN CRIME

A County Constabulary diary on the front parcel shelf and the Traffic Warden should have granted the vehicle the benefit of any doubt – providing the kiddy seat or sales literature was locked away in the boot.

Cars with radio telephones have, of course, a head start in Brown Wrapper Camouflage, especially if the radio aerial is the official RT type. CB radios and aerials, on the other hand, are a dead giveaway.

The success of BWC is enhanced by the model and colour of the car being camouflaged. White or Black are the best colours. Metallics are the worst – the police invariably go for utility finishes. Saloon cars are a must, but either two or four doors will do, unlike the USA. Sports cars are out.

Since the end of the Police Federation campaign, the subtleties of BWC have had to be re-examined.

Percy Nesbit uses two books which live on his back seat – the Constabulary Almanack and the Police Training Manual.

Arnold Lodge drives a black saloon, and opts for a chief inspector's cap, a pair of black gloves, a silver tipped swizzle stick and a spare black clip-on tie.

Alice Bradley drives a small white estate car. She sports a policewoman's bonnet, a fluorescent yellow net traffic over-jacket, two plastic road cones, a sign which reads ACCIDENT, a large first aid kit and a blue disco style flashing lamp (Inside only. It is most definitely illegal to sport a flashing blue lamp on a car roof, but reasonably okay to have a dead one sitting on the back seat or floor of the car).

The combinations for effective Brown Wrapper camouflage are practically endless.

Amorous Andy

Andy Randolph boasts that the cost of winning his bride was £370.

It was love at first sight. Even as the Traffic Warden stuck the parking ticket on his car windscreen, Andy knew she was the woman for him.

Thirty seven parking tickets and thirty six dozen red roses later, she agreed to marry him. Andy proposed while his Traffic Warden was writing out the thirty seventh ticket.

She said YES – but she still booked him.

Who says they're not on commission??

The Electric Town Car Revolution

At the time of publication of this book, the Sinclair C5 electric single seater town runabout, priced at around £400 on the road, presents a totally new side to the Traffic Warden game.

Having no registration number or road fund licence, where do the powers-that-be send the final demand for unpaid parking fines? How can they trace the owner?

In London, efforts to wheel clamp a Sinclair C5 can be thwarted simply by lifting the entire vehicle off the road at the clamped end and walking it away like a wheel barrow. And anyway, the standard issue wheel clamp doesn't fit a C5!

Doubtless, as Sinclair C5s flood our towns and clog our already over-crowded parking and no parking places, steps will be taken to resolve this new problem.

Traffic Wardens may be provided with a special parking ticket holder with secret adhesive that requires a release solvent only obtainable from the Clerk to the Justices on payment of the parking fine. But then we would undoubtedly see Sinclair C5s looking like far travelled suit cases.

A competitor to Sinclair might develop an electronic device for instantly flattening the C5's battery. Such a device, aimed like a space fiction ray gun at the C5 by a Traffic Warden, would represent awesome power. But then, the environmentalist lobby would undoubtedly have the device banned as a potential nuclear hazard. And anyway, the C5 driver can still pedal away!

No, the only current solution seems to be to carry the offending C5 away to the pound like a stray dog. We shall see.

KEEP CLEAR

PARKING VIOLATION

Refer to Road Traffic Act, Section 85—96

Town... S.o. A

Vehicle No... G.R.w 81G.H

Time... 23·25

This is not a parking ticket, but if it were within my power you would receive two; because of your bull-headed, inconsiderate, feeble attempt at parking, you have taken up enough room for a 20 mule team, two elephants, a goat and a safari of pygmies. The reason for giving you this ticket is so that in future you may think of someone else, other than yourself. Besides, I don't like domineering, egotistical or simple-minded drivers and you probably fit into one of these categories.

I sign off wishing you an early transmission failure
(preferable on the motorway at about 4.30 a.m.)
Also may the fleas of a thousand camels crawl up your exhaust.

Presents for Traffic Wardens

Earlier in this book we advised being nice to your local Traffic Wardens, with "pip and wave" techniques, etc.

Giving presents is a universally acceptable way of being nice – even if some of the presents are dreamed up a touch sadistically.

Ben Benson hates people who park their vehicles with no regard or concern for other drivers – too close so that it is impossible to escape or open the driver's door; taking up enough space for three vehicles; two feet out from the curb – this kind of performance is his pet hate. He carries around with him a pad of printed "PARKING VIOLATION" forms. One is illustrated on the left. Any vehicle qualifying for Ben's pet hate gets a parking ticket. (The author admits to having discovered Ben Benson's "present" by getting one of Ben's tickets himself!)

Ben's greatest pleasure is to be able to "book" a Traffic Warden's car. Being a salesman by profession, Ben is skilful when it comes to questioning techniques. He can be very nice to the Traffic Wardens he meets. "Good morning. Terrible weather we're having. Don't you wish you could do your job in your car instead of having to walk?"

"Haven't got a car. Don't drive!" So he can quit straight away.

"Would be nice, but no chance!" and Ben keeps going. "Where do you park your motor in this part of town? There's got to be a better place than I keep finding and who's going to know the best place if you don't?"

"Don't suppose you get much chance of using your car in this job. What do you drive? Had it long? What's the spec? My brother-in-law is looking for something like that."

Gerry Phipps runs his own printing business. He uses a different kind of pad, printed by his company and parcelled up into an individual one by one by six inch parcel. He delights in surprising Traffic Wardens he meets with "It's your Birthday. Here's a little gift from me and the rest of this town." But not when he's anywhere near his own car.

SCRIBBLING PAD FOR NARROW-MINDED BASTARDS

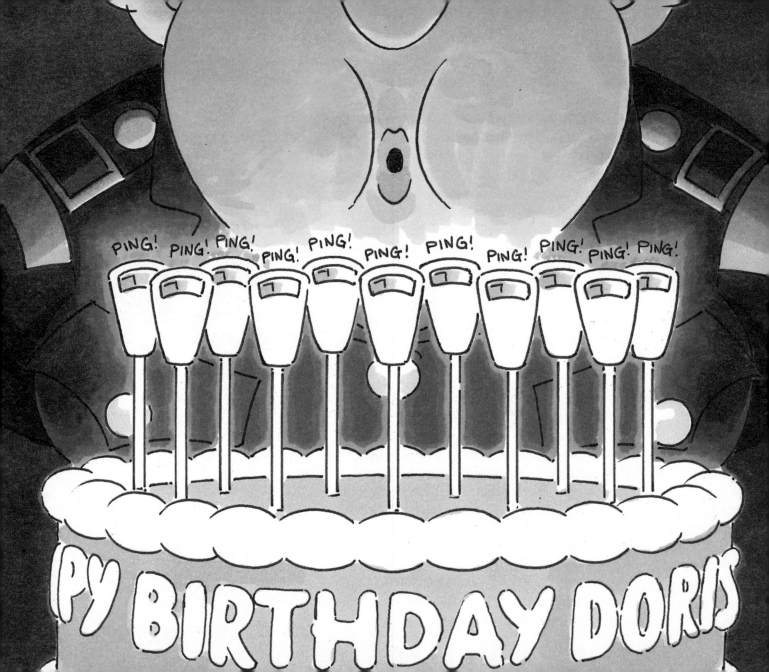

Finding out a Traffic Warden's real Birthday is as easy as finding out the Birthday of a receptionist or secretary if intentions are amourous or saleswise. Being nice to receptionists and secretaries is a stepping stone to the boss's office in selling.

"What's your star sign?"

"Taurus. Why do you want to know?"

"Thought it was. So's mine. What date in May?"

"Twentieth. Why?"

"Incredible. Don't you read your stars? Today's going to be a great day for both of us."

May twentieth goes into the salesman's records for that customer. Next May nineteenth, he sends off a Birthday card. The following morning he calls on the customer, to find the receptionist or secretary bending over backwards to please.

With Traffic Wardens, it's slightly more difficult. The questioner still has to discover the name and the address to send the Birthday card. So after the star sign questions ....

"What's your name?" Today is a "D" day for Tauruses"

"Gladys Horrocks. What do you mean, a D-day?"

"Tauruses whose names begin with a D hit the jackpot. Never mind. It's also good for street names. Where do you live?"

"Greville Road."

"No good again. It's got to be numbers then. Number 17 is today's best bet. How does that match?"

"28. What's that say?" Even the most atheistic star-unbeliever won't be able to resist such an enthusiastic, happy questioner.

So now the Traffic Warden can be sent Birthday cards. And Christmas cards. And Valentine's Day cards. And Father's Day cards. And presents through the post.

Genuinely "be nice" cards are easy to find. Illustrated in the following pages are some of the rarer varieties of not-quite-so-nice cards for Traffic Wardens.

I've been collecting presents all year for your Christmas Stocking

HOPE IT'S BIG ENOUGH....

.... FOR

a pair of lead soled shoes
*
a roll of non-stick sellotape
*
a packet of
well perished corn plasters
*
an exploding ball-point pen
*
a pair of no-way sunglasses
*
a tin of morphine-laced
slow down cough sweets
*
a year's supply of Number Nines,
labelled number tens
*
a one-way ticket to Russia
*
a bag of quick-drying cement

Food Parcels

It's not that Traffic Wardens are so poorly paid they need food parcels as the chosen present, it's more the fun to be had from certain "special" food delicacies.

We approach the end of this book. For readers who are sceptical as to the validity of the data it contains, attention must be called to two advertisements which appeared in the "Personal" columns of The Times, on April sixth, 1984.

> GLORIOUS SIXTH, TRAFFIC WARDEN
> SEASON STARTS TODAY.

And three advertisements further on .....

> SUCCULENT, PLUMP T/WARDENS WANTED.
> EPICURE QUALITY ONLY.
> HEDGEHOG HALL. WIRRAL.

Rumour has it that, following the great commercial success of Hedgehog flavoured crisps, a brand new flavour for the black market has been introduced – <u>Traffic Warden Flavour</u>.

Our researchers have so far failed to trace the suppliers of these new crisps, but investigations have led us to a master butcher working on a brand of sausage with continuous double yellow lines running along the skins. Most readers know, of course, why some Traffic Wardens have <u>two</u> yellow lines round their caps – so that drivers won't park on their heads!

This master butcher disclosed to our researchers the extent to which this new "sport" is spreading.

"Sheep stealing and horse knackering are now sports of the past for sausage, pie and pasty meat suppliers."

61

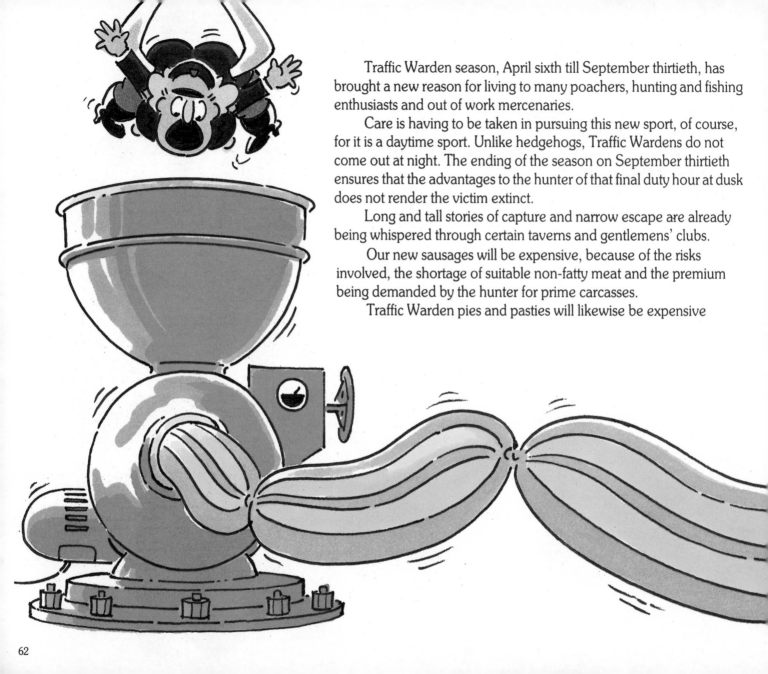

Traffic Warden season, April sixth till September thirtieth, has brought a new reason for living to many poachers, hunting and fishing enthusiasts and out of work mercenaries.

Care is having to be taken in pursuing this new sport, of course, for it is a daytime sport. Unlike hedgehogs, Traffic Wardens do not come out at night. The ending of the season on September thirtieth ensures that the advantages to the hunter of that final duty hour at dusk does not render the victim extinct.

Long and tall stories of capture and narrow escape are already being whispered through certain taverns and gentlemens' clubs.

Our new sausages will be expensive, because of the risks involved, the shortage of suitable non-fatty meat and the premium being demanded by the hunter for prime carcasses.

Traffic Warden pies and pasties will likewise be expensive

compared to the traditional steak and kidney or chicken and mushroom flavours, and also compared to the more exotic new brands of rabbit and prune and lamb and passion fruit."

Our researchers have finally uncovered that a prominent manufacturer of quality Christmas cakes, which are sent to customers all over the world in sealed tins, is planning to develop a Traffic Warden Fruit Cake for the next festive season.

The most recent survey has established that while this new under-cover market for Traffic Warden flavoured delicacies grows, several boroughs are now without Traffic Wardens at all.

Is this fear, we wonder, of the sheer weight of popular opinion against the wearers of that black and yellow uniform, or have the Traffic Wardens already been bagged by the hunters of Hedgehog Hall?

The borough constabularies decline to comment.

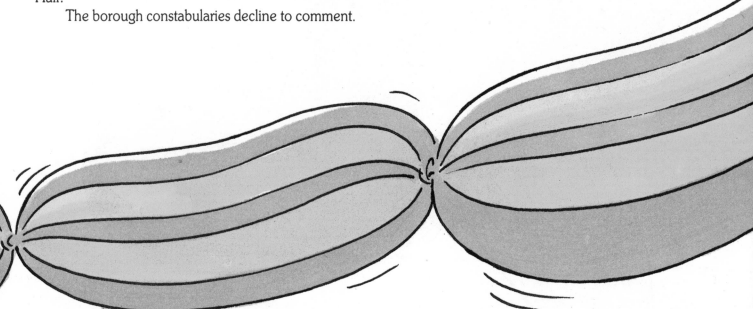

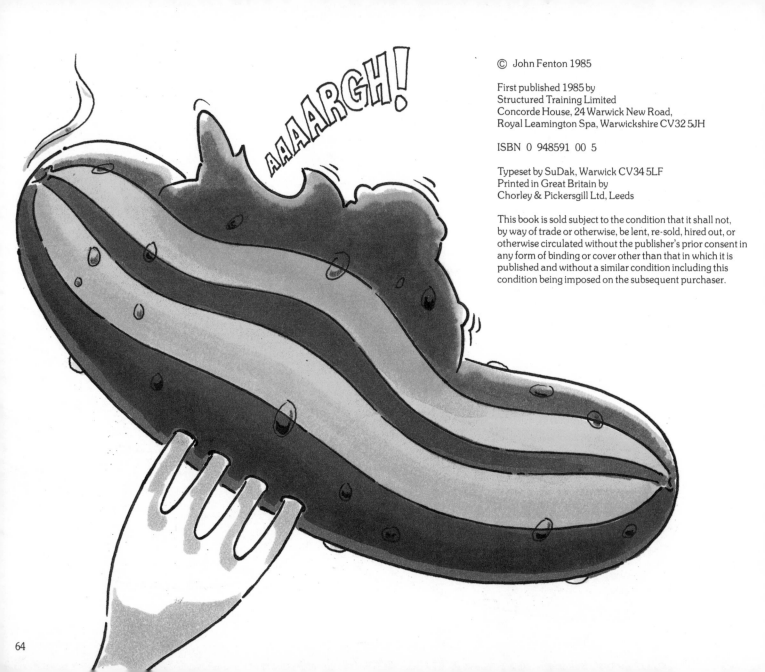

© John Fenton 1985

First published 1985 by
Structured Training Limited
Concorde House, 24 Warwick New Road,
Royal Leamington Spa, Warwickshire CV32 5JH

ISBN 0 948591 00 5

Typeset by SuDak, Warwick CV34 5LF
Printed in Great Britain by
Chorley & Pickersgill Ltd, Leeds